# Contents

Words in **bold** in the text can be found in the
Glossary on page 44.

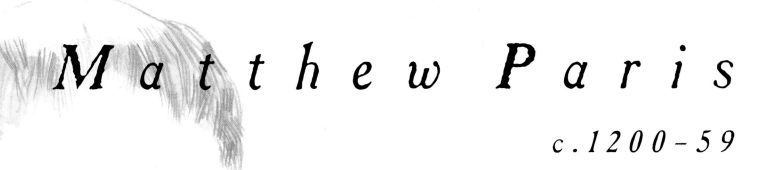

# *Matthew Paris*

## *c.1200–59*

*'He collected the deeds of great men from ancient times until the end of his own life, writing them down fully in his books, together with many marvellous events. Moreover, he was so skilled a workman in gold and silver, in carving and in painting, that he is believed to have left no equal in this world of the West.'*

This is a description of Matthew Paris, a **chronicler**, artist and craftsman, by a later chronicler called Thomas Walsingham. A chronicler was a cross between a historian and a newspaper reporter. Matthew wrote about the history of the world from its beginning, as described in the Bible. He also recorded, year by year, the events of his own time.

When young men became monks, they had the tops of their heads shaved. This hairstyle set them apart from ordinary people.

Like most chroniclers, Matthew was a **monk**. He spent most of his days in the scriptorium, or writing room, of St Albans Abbey. There he would sit, writing his books with a goose-quill pen, and decorating their margins with diagrams, maps and lively pictures of the many events he described.

We usually think of monks as men shut away from the world. But at St Albans, Matthew was right at the centre of things. The abbey was a stopping place on the Great North Road from London. It was used like a hotel by kings, nobles, travelling churchmen and important foreign visitors. Without leaving St Albans, Matthew could keep in touch with events all over Europe.

The first picture in Matthew's history includes a small self-portrait. He painted himself kneeling in prayer beneath the Virgin Mary and Jesus.

On rare occasions, he did leave the abbey. In 1248 he went to Norway to give advice on the running of a monastery. In 1255 he was in London, sketching a picture of an elephant. This strange animal was a present to King Henry III from the French king Louis IX. Always curious about anything unusual, Matthew wrote:

*'I do not think that an elephant had ever been seen before in England, and crowds flocked to gaze at such a novelty.'*

**OTHER CHRONICLERS**

**William of Malmesbury (1075–1143)**
– author of *The Deeds of the Kings of the English*.
**William of Newburgh (1135–1208)**
– author of the *History of England*.
**William Rishanger**
**John of Trakelowe**
**Henry of Blaneforde**
– later chroniclers at St Albans.

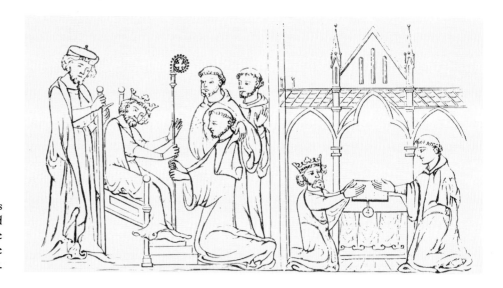

St Albans Abbey was founded by a king called Offa in the year 793. Here he hands the staff of office to the first abbot.

Matthew was the first person to draw a map of Britain in any detail. He shows rivers, towns and the important monasteries. St Albans is at the bottom, just above London.

Matthew was a lively story-teller, interested in scandal and gossip. He was not frightened of criticizing some of the most powerful people in England, including the king and the **Archbishop** of Canterbury. This archbishop, who was French, had got his job because he was the queen's uncle. Matthew always described him as a violent and greedy bully. According to Matthew, in 1250, the archbishop violently attacked a London priest:

*'He struck that holy man, a priest and a monk, with his fist as he stood in the middle of the church, beating him now on his aged breast, now on his grey-haired head and yelling, "This is how English traitors should be dealt with!" Raving horribly with unrepeatable oaths, he demanded that his sword should be brought to him.'*

Matthew would have been amazed to learn that he lived during what we now call the 'Middle Ages'. Like most chroniclers of the time, he believed that the world was coming to an end, as predicted in the Bible. He was always on the look-out for unusual events in nature, such as strange weather, eclipses, shooting stars, floods or earthquakes. To Matthew, these were all signs of the end of the world approaching. Here is a typical entry, from 1247:

*'In this same year, an earthquake was felt in various places in England, especially at London. It shook many buildings and was damaging and terrible. Earthquakes are unusual and unnatural in these western countries. It was therefore expected that the end of the ageing world was at hand, according to the threats of the Gospel.'*

In 1250, Matthew decided that he was getting too old to keep writing his chronicle, and he wrote a short verse to finish off that year's entry:

*'Matthew here your task is over,*
*Stop your pen and work no more.*
*Seek not what the future brings.*
*Another age has other things.'*

This typical page from Matthew's work describes the marriage of the German Emperor, Frederick, with Isabella, sister of Henry III of England. Matthew painted the bride and groom at the bottom.

After writing this verse, Matthew changed his mind. He continued working on the book until his death in 1259. Then another monk became the chronicler of St Albans. These are the first words that were written by the new chronicler:

*'Thus far wrote the venerable man, Brother Matthew Paris . . .*
*What has been added from this point may be ascribed to*
*another brother who, presuming to approach the works of so*
*great a predecessor, unworthy to continue, as he is unworthy to*
*undo his shoe, has not deserved to have even his name*
*mentioned on the page.'*

## DATE CHART

**c.1200**
**Matthew Paris is born.**

**1217**
**Becomes a monk at St Albans Abbey.**

**1236**
**Following the death of Roger of Wendover, the St Albans chronicler, Matthew begins to write the *Chronica Majora* (Great Chronicle).**

**1236–42**
**The Mongols invade Eastern Europe. Matthew records stories that have reached him about the new invaders.**

**1248**
**Matthew travels to Norway.**

**1248–50**
**King Louis of France fights a crusade, or holy war, against the Muslims of Egypt. Matthew reads reports from overseas and describes the war in his chronicle.**

**1255**
**Matthew travels to London to paint an elephant.**

**1259**
**Matthew dies.**

# Roger Bacon

## c.1214-92

'Machines may be made by which the largest ships, with only one man steering them, will be moved faster than if they were filled by rowers. Wagons may be built which will move with incredible speed and without the aid of beasts. Flying machines can be made in which a man may beat the air with wings like a bird. Machines will make it possible to go to the bottom of seas and rivers.'

These predictions were made by a **friar** and a teacher called Roger Bacon. He was describing some of the wonders that might be brought about by the study of science. In his own lifetime, most people would have laughed at Bacon's predictions as wild fantasy. But how many of them have come true?

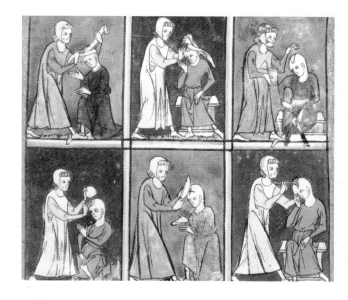

Bacon wrote about medical science, which was very basic in the Middle Ages. These painful images of head operations come from a thirteenth-century book on surgery.

Bacon studied the
night sky and wrote
about the stars in
his book. Like most
educated men of the
time, he believed in
astrology – the idea
that the stars
influence life on Earth.

Bacon wrote a huge book called the *Opus Majus* (Great Work).
This was a survey of the level of people's knowledge in Europe. He
looked at one science after another, suggesting ways in which each could
be improved. For example, he argued that scholars should learn other
languages as well as their own, such as Greek and Arabic:

*'Almost all the secrets of **philosophy** lie hidden in foreign
languages. Great secrets of the sciences and of the arts showing
the hidden things of nature have not yet been translated.'*

He also recommended practical experiments. To be a scientist, he said, you needed to study nature as well as books.

Bacon was a bold and original thinker. This is what he said about crusades, the Christian holy wars fought against people of other religions:

*'War does not work against unbelievers. Those who survive, together with their children, are simply made more bitter towards the Christian faith.'*

Before Bacon's time, the Church encouraged people to set off on holy wars against people of other religions. Bacon wanted to spread the Christian faith, but not by war.

## OTHER SCHOLARS

**Adelard of Bath
(c.1090–1150)**
– translated Arabic writings on astronomy into Latin.

**Robert of Chester
(c.1100–50s)**
– translated Arabic writings on mathematics into Latin.

**John of Salisbury
(c.1115–80)**
– Bishop of Chartres and a writer on politics and logic.

**Robert Grossetete
('Great Head')
(c.1168–1253)**
– Bishop of Lincoln, a mathematician and a translator of Greek writers.

**John Duns Scotus
(c.1265–1308)**
– a Scottish philosopher.

**William of Ockham
(c.1300–49)**
– a philosopher and writer on logic.

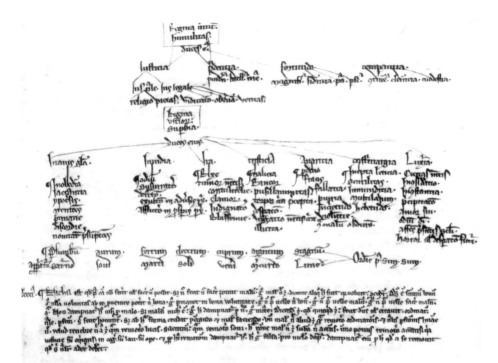

In Western Europe, scholars all spoke and wrote in Latin – the language of this description of the planets and different metals. This helped scientists like Bacon to swap ideas with many other European scholars.

## DATE CHART

**c.1214**
Roger Bacon is born in Somerset.

**1227**
Begins to study at Oxford University.

**1234–50**
Studies and teaches at the University of Paris.

**1250**
Returns to Oxford to teach.

**c.1257**
Becomes a Franciscan friar.

**1257–67**
Bacon's ideas get him into trouble with the Franciscan authorities. He is kept under close watch in the Franciscan house at Paris for ten years.

**1266–8**
Gets the support of the new Pope, Clement IV. Writes the *Opus Majus* (Great Work) for him.

**1268**
Allowed to return to Oxford, where he writes a book on philosophy.

**1277–92**
Bacon gets into trouble again with the head of the Franciscans. For almost fifteen years he is kept a prisoner in Paris.

**1292–4**
Free again, Bacon spends his last two years at Oxford writing a book on theology (the study of religion).

Bacon's ideas got him into trouble with the religious authorities. They accused him of 'novelties', or new ideas. The **Catholic Church** was often against 'novelties'. It believed that everything that people needed to know was in the Bible. Bacon was a firm Christian, but he knew that the Bible did not explain everything.

After his death, Bacon got a reputation as a man with sinister magical powers. He was said to have built a talking bronze head which could predict the future. It was not until the *Opus Majus* was first printed, in 1733, that people could find out what Roger Bacon was really like.

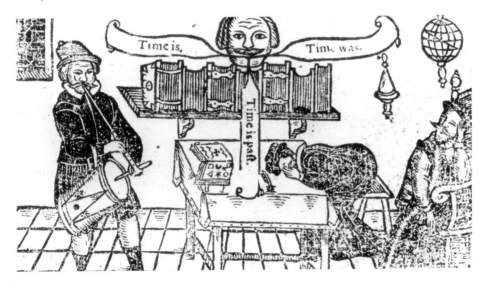

For many years, people thought of Bacon as a magician. In this drawing from the 1590s, he is asleep in his study while his magic brass head is speaking.

13

# R o b e r t   B r u c e

## 1274 – 1329

*'It was an evil, miserable and calamitous day for the English ...
When the two armies joined battle, the great English horses
charged on to the Scottish **pikes**, which bristled like a dense
forest. There arose a great and terrible crash of splintering
pikes and of horses wounded to death ... Bannockburn was
spoken about for many years afterwards in English throats.'*

This is a description of the most famous battle in Scottish history. It was
written by an English monk from Lanercost, close to the Scottish border.
To the monk, the defeat of the English at Bannockburn in 1314 was a
terrible disaster. But to the Scots, the battle was a triumph which
confirmed their faith in their leader, Robert Bruce, as a national hero.

A statue of Robert Bruce at
Stirling Castle. Bruce won the
Battle of Bannockburn, his
greatest victory, outside this
castle.

14

Fighting between the Scots and the English was common throughout the Middle Ages. The English had won many battles, especially during the reign of King Edward I (1272–1307), nicknamed the 'Hammer of the Scots'.

Edward had conquered Wales in the 1280s, and he planned to add Scotland to his kingdom. In 1296 he led his army north and captured the Scottish king, John Balliol. Edward took him back to England, together with the Stone of Scone. Scotland's rulers had always been crowned sitting on this sacred stone. By taking it, Edward hoped to make sure there would be no more Scottish kings.

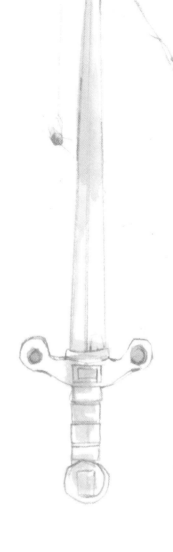

In Westminster Abbey, King Edward I had a new oak coronation chair made to hold the Stone of Scone. All but two of England's rulers since then have been crowned sitting on this chair, above the Scottish stone.

However, many Scottish nobles refused to accept English rule. Led by William Wallace, they organized a great uprising. For ten months, Wallace ruled Scotland on behalf of John Balliol. But in 1305, Edward went north, beat the Scots again and put Wallace to death. His body, chopped into pieces, was displayed around Scotland as a warning to rebels.

The next year, the Scots tried again. Unlike Wallace, their new leader, Robert Bruce, had royal blood and it was his **birthright** to claim the throne. On 25 March 1306, his followers crowned him King of Scotland at Scone Abbey.

## OTHERS TO STUDY

**David II (1324–71)**
– son of Robert Bruce and King of Scotland from 1329.
**Sir James Douglas (1286–1330)**
– a powerful supporter of Bruce in his campaigns against the English.
**Robert II (1316–90)**
– Robert Bruce's grandson, and the first Stewart (or Stuart) ruler of Scotland.

In 1306, Robert Bruce had only a tiny army and many enemies. As well as the English, he had to fight against fellow Scots who still thought John Balliol should be king. Bruce was quickly defeated and forced to escape to the islands in the west of Scotland.

A famous story was later told about this time. Bruce was said to have watched a spider trying to fix its web to a roof beam. Six times the spider failed, but on the seventh it succeeded. The example of the spider taught Bruce not to give up.

In 1307, Bruce returned to the mainland and started a new campaign. This time, instead of risking open battles, his men made surprise raids. When they captured a fortress, they destroyed it so that it could not be used again by the English.

Bruce's luck finally changed with the death of Edward I, on 7 July 1307. The new king, Edward II, was not interested in fighting. While Edward stayed in England, Bruce was able to beat his Scottish enemies one by one. By 1314, most of the English castles in southern Scotland had also been captured by the Scottish king.

When Bruce laid **siege** to Stirling Castle, the most important fortress in Scotland, Edward was forced to fight. He raised a huge army of 20,000 men and rode north. Bruce had only 5,500 men, but he planned carefully for the battle. He placed his troops between the River Forth and a deep ditch called the Bannock Burn. If the English attacked, they would have to fight in a narrow, boggy area where their numbers would not help them.

## DATE CHART

**1274**
11 June: Robert Bruce is born at Turnberry Castle, Ayr.

**1296**
Edward I of England invades Scotland and captures King John Balliol.

**1297**
The Scots, led by William Wallace, rebel against Edward.

**1298**
Edward defeats Wallace at the Battle of Falkirk.

**1305**
Edward captures and kills Wallace.

**1306**
Robert Bruce is crowned at Scone as King of Scotland. He is defeated at the battles of Methven and Dalry. He kills Balliol's nephew, John ('the Red') Comyn and escapes to the western islands.

**1307**
Bruce starts a new campaign in Scotland. Edward I dies.

**1308–9**
Bruce defeats his Scottish rivals.

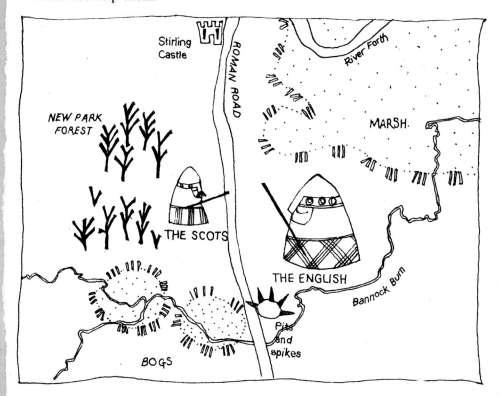

Edward fell into Bruce's trap and the English army was defeated. The Lanercost monk explained what the victory at Bannockburn meant:

*'After the aforesaid victory, Robert Bruce was commonly called King of Scotland by all men, because he had acquired Scotland by force of arms.'*

To be a proper king in the Middle Ages, you needed the backing of the Church, headed by the Pope. But the Pope, John XXII, refused to agree that Bruce was king, because Bruce had killed John Comyn, Balliol's nephew, in a church in 1306. In 1320, thirty-nine Scottish nobles sent a letter to the Pope, the famous *Declaration of Arbroath*, to make him change his mind:

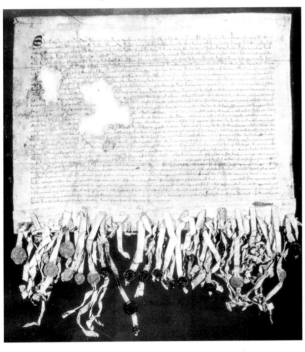

The *Declaration of Arbroath*, with the seals of the Scottish nobles dangling at the bottom.

*'For as long as a hundred of us remain alive, we will never on any conditions be brought under English rule. It is in truth not for glory, nor riches, nor honours that we are fighting, but for freedom – for that alone, which an honest man will only give up with his life.'*

In 1324, the Pope finally accepted that Robert Bruce was the true King of Scotland. However Edward II refused to make peace. It was not until he was murdered in 1327 that the war came to an end. His son, Edward III, conceded that Scotland was a free and independent nation.

As for the sacred Stone of Scone, it is still in Westminster Abbey, where King Edward I placed it seven hundred years ago.

**1312–14**
Bruce captures the English castles in southern Scotland.

**1314**
Edward II invades Scotland and is defeated at the Battle of Bannockburn (23–24 June).

**1320**
*Declaration of Arbroath*. Scottish nobles ask the Pope to give Bruce his backing.

**1322**
Bruce raids England and defeats Edward in Yorkshire.

**1324**
The Pope recognizes Bruce as King of Scotland.

**1327**
Edward II is murdered by his wife and her lover.

**1328**
The new English king, Edward III, accepts Scottish independence.

**1329**
Bruce dies in his castle at Cardross.

# John Wycliffe

## c.1328-84

*'He took the Gospel, handed down by Christ to the learned men of the Church, and translated it from Latin into English. In this way it became open to **laymen** and badly educated women. This was like scattering pearls to be trodden underfoot by swine.'*

Henry of Knighton, the chronicler who wrote these words, was talking about John Wycliffe. Wycliffe was a university teacher who had attacked the power of the Church and argued that ordinary people should be allowed to read the Bible. To churchmen like Henry, this was a really shocking idea.

Wycliffe criticized monks and friars. As this picture shows, he saw them as greedy animals, who became rich from living off ordinary people.

### IMPORTANT LOLLARDS

Nicholas of Hereford
(died c.1420)
– worked with Wycliffe on the first English Bible.
Sir John Oldcastle
(1378–1417)
– a leader of the Lollards, who was hanged by Henry V.

The opening page of the *Book of Acts*, from the Wycliffe English Bible. This beautifully decorated copy must have been owned by someone very wealthy.

## DATE CHART

**c.1328**
John Wycliffe is born in Yorkshire.

**1340s**
Begins his education at Oxford University.

**1370**
Wycliffe becomes a Doctor of Theology at Oxford University.

**1373**
Edward III is too sick and old to rule. His eldest son, the Black Prince, is also ill. Another son, John of Gaunt, becomes the most powerful man in the country.

**1376**
Death of the Black Prince. Wycliffe writes that the Church should not own property. Employed by John of Gaunt, who wants England to stop paying taxes to the Pope.

**1377**
Death of Edward III. Richard II, ten-year-old son of the Black Prince, is crowned king. Wycliffe is ordered by the Bishop of London to defend his views at a trial in St Paul's Cathedral, London. John of Gaunt uses soldiers to break up the trial. Wycliffe's writings are condemned by Pope Gregory XI.

**1378**
Wycliffe is tried a second time. He is protected by the king's mother, Joan of Kent.

**1381**
Wycliffe loses his job at Oxford, mainly because of his support for the Peasants' Revolt, but continues to write books. His attacks on the Church and the Pope get even stronger. He starts a translation of the Bible into English, finished by others after his death.

**1384**
Dies of a heart attack.

Nowadays, it is hard to realize just how powerful the Church was in the Middle Ages. There was only one official religion in western Europe, that of the Catholic Church, headed by the Pope. Everyone had to pay a tax to the Church, called a tithe. The Pope received five times as much money in taxes from England as the king did. The Church had the power to arrest and try people as **heretics**.

**Priests** were believed to have special powers. For example, it was said that they could forgive people's sins, saving them from going to hell. Priests told people what to believe and how to behave.

At first, Wycliffe simply criticized the wealth of the Church. This brought him to the attention of John of Gaunt, the most powerful English nobleman. He wanted England to stop paying taxes to the Pope, so he gave Wycliffe his protection.

Wycliffe went on to attack the teachings of the Church. He argued that all Christians were equal – the Pope and the priests were no closer to God than ordinary believers and had no special powers. Instead of listening to the teachings of priests, people should be allowed to read the Bible. Wycliffe began to translate the book into English.

After his death, many people were influenced by Wycliffe. His followers were called **'Lollards'** ('mutterers'). In the 1400s, about one hundred of them were burned alive as heretics. But Wycliffe's ideas continued to spread.

# *W a t   T y l e r*

## *? - 1 3 8 1*

*'They set off and went towards London. They were a full sixty thousand and their chief captain was one Wat Tyler. He was a tiler of roofs, and a wicked and nasty fellow he was.'*

This is how a French writer, Jean Froissart, described the amazing events that took place in the summer of 1381. For a few days in June, the government of England was at the mercy of an army of **peasants**, led by a man called Wat Tyler.

King Richard II was only ten years old when he was crowned, in 1377.

Peasants were expected to look up to the nobles, and show great respect, like this man raising his hat to a lady.

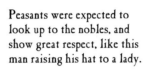

Froissart believed that everyone had a natural place in society which was decided by God. It was God's will that kings ruled and peasants obeyed them. So he was horrified that peasants should rise up against their king. All the writers of the time shared Froissart's views. They all thought that Wat Tyler must have been a 'wicked and nasty fellow'. This makes it impossible for us to find out what Tyler was really like.

However, we can try to find out why Tyler and his army marched on London. In the 1340s, a terrible plague, the Black Death, had killed a third of the people of England. There were fewer peasants to do the work and they wanted higher wages. But the government passed laws to keep wages low and to stop peasants from moving freely about the country. In the 1370s, the poet William Langland wrote:

*'And so it is nowadays – the labourer is angry unless he gets higher wages, and he curses the day that ever he was born a workman. He blames God, and murmurs against Reason, and curses the King and his Council for making laws to plague the workman!'*

One group of peasants was not paid wages at all. They were the **villeins**, who were forced to work for their lord in return for the right to grow their own food. These peasants wanted their freedom.

### OTHER REBELS

**John Ball (?–1381)**
– an ex-priest who was one of the leaders of the Kentish rebels.
**Jack Cade (?–1450)**
– leader of another Kent uprising, in 1450.
**Jack Straw (?–1381)**
– Tyler's second-in-command, beheaded in London.

21

This French painting of the Peasants' Revolt shows Wat Tyler, on the left, and the priest John Ball, on horseback. The peasants would have looked much more ragged than these men in shiny armour.

According to Froissart, a Kent priest called John Ball began to preach a new kind of sermon to the peasants:

*'Things cannot go well in England until everything is owned by all the people together, and there is no difference between gentlefolk and peasants. We all come from the same father and mother, Adam and Eve. How then can they say that they are greater than us, except by making us work to produce the wealth that they spend?'*

In 1377–81, the government introduced three new taxes to pay for the war against France. This war, which had been dragging on since 1337, was very unpopular. The taxes were particularly hated because they were poll taxes – poor people had to pay the same amount as the rich. This is what finally drove the peasants into rebellion.

In June 1381, the tax collectors were attacked in Kent and Essex. Then the peasants began to gather together, armed with anything they could lay their hands on. In Kent, an army of peasants marched on Rochester and Maidstone. Wat Tyler came forward as their leader – he had probably served as a soldier in France and been chosen because he knew about fighting.

The peasant armies from Essex and Kent each made their way to London. The fourteen-year-old King Richard II and his advisors were taken by surprise. The rebels opened prisons and burned down the houses of the most hated ministers. They forced their way into the **Tower of London**, where they killed the **Chancellor** and the **Treasurer** – the men held responsible for the poll taxes.

22

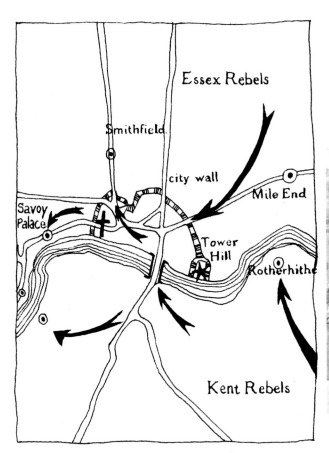

This map shows the route taken by the peasants during the revolt.

Wat Tyler is cut down by the mayor, in front of King Richard (below). On the right, the young king is shown again, calming the angry peasants.

On 14 June, King Richard rode to Smithfield to meet Wat Tyler. It is not clear exactly what happened, but there was probably a quarrel, and Tyler was stabbed and killed by William Walworth, the mayor of London. When they saw this, the peasants got ready to attack. However, the king managed to calm them down. According to the chronicler Thomas Walsingham, this is what he said:

*'Surely you do not wish to fire on your own king? I will be your captain and your leader. Follow me into that field where you can have all the things you would like to ask for.'*

Richard agreed to all the peasants' demands and he said that the villeins would get their freedom. The rebels went home and the revolt was over. Afterwards, the king broke the promises he had made. But there were no more attempts to collect the poll tax.

For hundreds of years, Wat Tyler was remembered as a wicked man. In the eighteenth century, his reputation began to change. Some writers and thinkers began to argue that people were equal after all. One writer, Tom Paine, even suggested that a statue of Tyler should be put up at Smithfield. He said that the peasant leader was a hero for fighting against an unfair tax.

**13 June:** King Richard goes to Rotherhithe by barge to try to talk to the Kent rebels, without success. The peasants break into the city, setting fire to several buildings, including John of Gaunt's palace, the Savoy.

**14 June:** Richard meets a combined group of rebels at Mile End. He agrees to their demands. The rebels seize three of the king's ministers and behead them on Tower Hill.

**15 June:** Richard meets Wat Tyler at Smithfield. There is probably a quarrel in which William Walworth, the mayor, stabs Tyler and kills him. Richard manages to calm the peasants and they agree to go home.

**27 June–20 July:** Execution of the rebel leaders, including John Ball.

# Henry Yeveley

## c.1320–1400

*'We went to the city of Lichfield, where there is a most lovely church dedicated to St Chad. It is of wondrous beauty, having very high steeples, and is finely adorned and enriched with paintings, carvings and other church fittings.'*

This is a description of Lichfield **Cathedral** by an Irish friar, who visited the city in 1323. In many parts of Britain you can still see stone buildings, such as castles and cathedrals, that were built during the Middle Ages. Have you ever wondered who made them and how they did it?

Masons at work, shaping stones, mixing mortar and hoisting it up in buckets.

The builders were called masons, and they had to carve every block of stone by hand, using chisels and hammers. The architects who designed the buildings were called master masons.

For forty years, from 1360 to 1400, Henry Yeveley was the most important builder in Britain. He was the king's own master mason. His work included the design of every kind of building, from a stone bridge to a cathedral. He also built **fortifications**, such as castles and city walls. On a smaller scale, he designed stone tombs for the royal family.

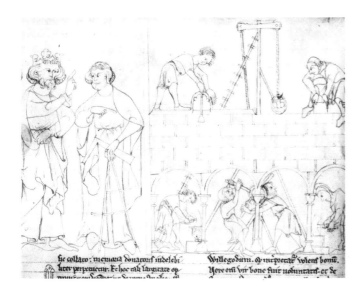

A master mason, holding his drawing instruments, shows a king around a building site. The masons look like they're working extra hard for the occasion!

As a master mason, Yeveley had many different skills. Most importantly, he was a designer who drew plans for buildings. He made small-scale drawings on **parchment**. At the building site, he scratched full-sized drawings on a plaster floor. These 'tracing floor' drawings were used to make templates – shapes cut out of board which acted as guides for the stone carvers.

Yeveley was also a contractor, getting the building materials and hiring the workers, and a foreman, giving orders to his masons and checking the quality of their work. Finally, he was also a skilled stone carver, able to work on any part of the building if necessary.

It took many years to develop all these different skills. As a young **apprentice**, Yeveley learned to carve stone and to draw. In his twenties he became a 'journeyman' mason, travelling the country to work on different jobs. Only the most skilled journeymen rose to be master masons themselves.

The most ambitious building that any master mason could work on was a cathedral. Cathedrals were the biggest buildings constructed during the Middle Ages. They were made to honour God, so they had to be as beautiful and impressive as possible.

**OTHER BUILDERS**

**Hugh Herland (working 1360–1405)** – a master carpenter who often worked with Yeveley.
**William Ramsay (working 1386–49)** – a master mason who designed the first buildings in the perpendicular style.
**William Wynford (working 1360–1404)** – a master mason who designed New College, Oxford.

25

In some cathedrals, you can find stone portraits of master masons. This is Henry Wy, who worked at St Albans Abbey in the 1320s.

Styles of cathedral building changed over the years. At first, cathedrals had thick pillars and small windows with rounded arches. As building methods improved, the masons were able to design more delicate pillars, bigger windows with pointed arches, and higher and higher ceilings.

When Yeveley was a child, cathedrals were built in a style called 'decorated'. This style was rich and complicated, with lots of flowing curves. Yeveley and the builders of his generation preferred a simpler design, now known as 'perpendicular' (upright), with straight lines and huge windows. The aim was to give people a feeling of vast space.

This is Yeveley's greatest work, the huge nave of Canterbury Cathedral, with its soaring pillars. Imagine what it must have felt like to stand here in the early 1400s, with the singing of the monks echoing around the walls and ceiling.

You can see this style best at Canterbury Cathedral, where Yeveley designed the nave – the part of the church where ordinary people stood to listen to the services, which were sung by monks. In the 1390s, Yeveley pulled down the old, badly lit nave and rebuilt it in the new perpendicular style. He made great windows, to let the light stream in, and straight pillars which soar twenty-five metres up to the ceiling. This nave is Yeveley's masterpiece, and he made it when he was in his seventies.

Yeveley died before the nave was finished. Almost to the end, he was working on various projects, including a great new banqueting hall for King Richard II at Westminster and a stone tomb for the king in Westminster Abbey. As well as this designing work, he had another business supplying building materials to other masons. By the time of his death, in 1400, he had become a very wealthy man.

This bronze statue of King Edward III in Westminster Abbey rests on his tomb, designed by Henry Yeveley in 1377.

# Geoffrey Chaucer

## c. 1340 – 1400

*'Whan that Aprille with his shoures soote*
*The droghte of March hath perced to the roote...'*

*(When April, with his sweet showers,*
*Has pierced the drought of March to the root...)*

These are the opening lines of one of the most famous poems in the English language, Geoffrey Chaucer's *The Canterbury Tales*. This is a collection of stories told by a group of **pilgrims** as they ride from London to Canterbury Cathedral.

The stained-glass windows of Canterbury Cathedral show scenes of pilgrims, on their way to the famous shrine.

The opening lines set the scene. It is spring. Flowers are beginning to bloom and birds to sing. Spring makes people restless:

*'Thanne longen folk to goon on pilgrimages…
And specially from every shires ende
Of Engelond to Caunterbury they wend.'*

*(Then folk long to go on pilgrimages…
And specially, from every shire's end of England,
They make their way to Canterbury.)*

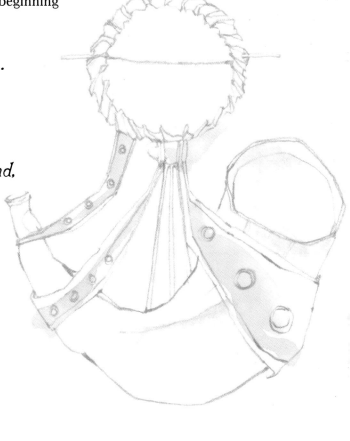

Thomas Becket was an Archbishop of Canterbury who was murdered in the cathedral in 1170. The monks saved some of his blood. Heavily watered down, it was given to pilgrims who visited his shrine.

Canterbury Cathedral held the tomb of **Saint Thomas Becket** and it was the most popular place in Britain for pilgrimages. People believed that the saint had great power to help them. He could cure illnesses and bring good luck. Going on a pilgrimage could help you get to heaven. It was also a good excuse for a holiday.

## OTHER BRITISH POETS

William Langland (c.1331–99)
– author of *Piers the Ploughman.*
The unknown author of *Gawain and the Green Knight* (1370s)
John Gower (1330–1408)
– author of three long poems in French, Latin and English.
Thomas Hoccleve (c.1370–1450)
– author of *The Regiment of Princes.*
John Lydgate (c.1370–1452)
– author of *The Troy Book,* and many other poems.

Pilgrimages brought people together from all groups in society – rich and poor, male and female. Among Chaucer's thirty pilgrims we meet a knight, a doctor, a friar, a nun, a miller, a merchant, a cook and a sea captain. This wide range gives us a wonderful picture of life in the fourteenth century.

The pilgrims are described in vivid detail. This is how Chaucer introduces his miller:

*'His berd as any sowe or fox was reed*
*And thereto brood, as though it were a spade.*
*Upon the cop right of his nose he hade*
*A werte, and theron stood a tuft of herys.'*

*(His beard was as red as a sow*
*or a fox, and broad as a spade.*
*On the top of his nose he had a wart,*
*and on it stood a tuft of hairs.)*

The miller plays the bagpipes as the pilgrims set off for Canterbury.

To pass the time on their journey, the pilgrims decide to tell each other stories. The best tale will win a prize – a free supper at Canterbury, paid for by everyone else.

This framework allowed Chaucer to include many different types of story, drawn from all over Europe. There are religious stories and love stories, funny stories and sad stories. *The Nun's Priest's Tale* is all about a cock and a hen. *The Parson's Tale*, which comes last, is not a story at all, but a sermon on the seven deadly sins.

For most of the Middle Ages, wealthy English people spoke French as their first language and listened to French poetry. Chaucer himself was a court poet who understood French. However, he chose to write his poems in English. This shows that a big change was taking place in the higher ranks of society. In the late 1300s, more and more nobles were speaking English. This might have been because England was at war with France. French was the language of the enemy.

For three hundred years, pilgrims climbed these steps to the shrine of St Thomas Becket. You can see the hollows worn by their feet.

By writing in English rather than French, Chaucer could reach a much wider audience. Although he wrote *The Canterbury Tales* for nobles, it quickly became popular with a wide range of people. In the 1470s, it was one of the first books to be printed by William Caxton (see pages 42–3).

Chaucer also had a big influence on other poets. A younger poet, John Lydgate, looked up to him as the 'father of English poetry', the first writer to 'rain the gold dewdrops of speech' into the English language:

*'Since he in English making was the best,*
*Pray unto God to give his soul good rest.'*

The Martyrdom Transcept at Canterbury Cathedral. This is the place where St Thomas Becket was murdered.

# Juliana of Norwich

## c. 1342 – after 1416

*'The Fiend had me by the
throat, putting his face very
near mine. It was like a young
man's face, and long and very
lean. I never saw the like. The
colour was red as a tile, and
there were black spots like
freckles … He grinned at me
slyly, showing white teeth,
which made it, I thought, all the
more horrible. There was no
proper shape to his body or
hands, but with his paws he held
me by the throat and would
have strangled me if he could.
But all the time I went on
trusting I would be saved by
the mercy of God.'*

In the Middle Ages, people believed
that the world was a battlefield
where the Devil struggled with Jesus
Christ for the souls of men and
women. To Juliana of Norwich, who
wrote the words above, the Fiend, or
the Devil, was just as real as the
room in which she lived.

People thought of the Devil as a hideous monster, but he could appear in many different forms. In this picture he is dressed as a woman. It's not a very convincing disguise!

Juliana (or Julian) was a **mystic**. Mystics are known in many religions all over the world. They are people who have **visions** in which they believe that they are in contact with their god or gods.

The mystic usually has to get into a certain state of mind before having a vision. Going without food or sleep are common methods. Juliana had her visions while she was suffering from a serious illness in 1373. She had been lying in bed for several days, certain she was dying. Suddenly, she saw in front of her a crown of thorns with blood dripping from it. This was just the beginning of a series of strange visions, or 'showings', as Juliana called them.

Juliana was lying on her sick-bed when she saw her first strange vision. This picture comes from an English prayer book, painted in East Anglia in the 1340s.

## OTHER MYSTICS

**Richard Rolle (1300–49)** – author of *The Fire of Love.* **Walter Hilton (died 1396)** – author of *The Ladder of Perfection.*

33

The first page of Juliana's book, the earliest written in English by a woman.

Juliana believed that her visions had been sent to teach her something, and she spent years praying and thinking about what it could be. Finally, she wrote about her visions in a book called *Revelations of Divine Love*, the first known book written by an English woman. In this book, she concluded that God had sent the visions as a sign of his love.

Juliana was able to spend years thinking about her visions because she was an anchoress. That means that she chose for religious reasons to be shut away from normal life and live in a cell called an anchorhold. In the 1300s, there were anchorholds all over Britain, often attached to a church. You can still see some anchorholds today.

No one thought there was anything strange about being an anchoress. In fact, anchoresses relied on people in the outside world to support them with money. People often left money in their wills to them, hoping that their prayers would help those people get to heaven.

There was even a popular guidebook for anchoresses, called the *Ancrene Wisse*. Written in the 1200s, it is full of practical advice:

*'My dear sisters, unless you are driven by need, you must not keep any animal except a cat. It is a hateful thing, Christ knows, when complaints are made in the village about an anchoress's livestock. If you need to keep a cow, make sure it does not bother anyone. An anchoress ought not to have anything that draws her heart outwards.'*

There was a solemn ceremony when a woman became an anchoress. It included a procession to the cell, which was blessed by the bishop. The anchoress was sprinkled with holy water and invited to enter. Then the door was sealed up for good. It was like a funeral.

Juliana spent her life in a cell at St Julian's Church, Norwich. However, she was not completely cut off. She had two servants, Sarah and Alice, who did the shopping and cooked her meals. She also had a window into the church, so that she could hear the services, and another window on to the street, so that she could speak to visitors. Many people came to see her to ask for her advice. Everyone respected her for the life she had chosen to lead.

This is St Julian's Church, Norwich, where Juliana lived as an anchoress. The photograph shows a modern side-chapel, built on the site of the anchorhold. Juliana took her name from the church; her original name is not known.

# Owain Glyndwr

## c.1350 – c.1415

*'Strange wonders were reported at the birth of this man, for the night he was born, all his father's horses in the stable were found to stand up to their bellies in blood.'*

The man described here, by an English chronicler, Raphael Holinshed, was Owain Glyndwr, the leader of the last big Welsh rising against English rule. Between 1400 and 1404, Owain made himself ruler of the whole of Wales. King Henry IV sent three **expeditions** to beat Owain, but they all failed.

This nineteenth-century picture shows Owain sitting on his throne. No one knows what he really looked like.

### OTHERS TO STUDY

**Owain Cyfeiliog (1130–1197)**
– a prince and poet.
**Gerald of Wales (1147–1223)**
– author of *A Journey Through Wales* and *A Description of Wales.*
**Llewelyn ap Gruffudd, Prince of Wales (ruled 1258–1282)**
– the last independent ruler of Wales, killed by the English in 1282.

English people thought that the Welsh leader must have had strange magical powers. Holinshed wrote:

*'Through magic, it was thought, Owain caused such foul weather of winds, tempest, rain, snow and hail to be raised, to annoy the king's army, that the king was forced to return home.'*

The real reason for Owain's success was that he avoided big battles. Like Robert Bruce, he preferred to make surprise raids and then escape back up into the mountains. Henry, who also had English rebels to deal with, could not afford to keep troops in Wales for any length of time because it was expensive to keep an army fed and paid.

Owain had big plans for Wales, including a Welsh Parliament and Welsh universities. He made treaties with the English rebels, the French and the Scots. With their help, Owain even planned to conquer part of England.

Owain's plans came to nothing. Once Henry had defeated his English enemies, he was able to concentrate on reconquering Wales. The anonymous Welsh *Annals of Owain Glyndwr* finish with these words:

*'1415. Owain went into hiding on St Matthew's Day, and thereafter his hiding place was unknown. Very many say that he died. The wise men say that he did not.'*

In Welsh legend, Owain is said to be sleeping in a cave, waiting for another chance to fight the English. Today his memory is kept alive by Welsh nationalists, people who want Wales to have its own government rather than be governed by Britain. One group of nationalists is called the *Meibion Glyndwr*, the sons of Glyndwr.

**DATE CHART**

**1276–84**
Edward I of England conquers Wales.

**c.1350**
Owain Glyndwr is born.

**1399**
Richard II is overthrown by his cousin, who becomes Henry IV.

**1400**
After quarrelling with an English neighbour, Owain decides to fight against Henry. 16 September: Owain is proclaimed Prince of Wales by his followers. Raids English lands in north-east Wales. King Henry leads an army against him, but cannot find him.

**1401**
Henry again fails to stop the uprising. Owain now controls the whole of north Wales.

**1402**
Owain's revolt spreads to central and south-east Wales. English settlers in Wales are forced to take shelter in castles and walled towns.

**1404**
Owain captures Harlech and Aberystwyth castles and now rules Wales. Calls a Welsh parliament at Machynlleth. Makes a treaty with King Charles VI of France, who sends troops to Wales.

**1405**
Owain and two English nobles agree to divide England between them. But Henry defeats the English rebels and then wins his first victories against Owain.

**1406–12**
Henry reconquers Wales.

**1412**
Owain and a small band are last heard of, making raids in north-west Wales.

# M a r g e r y  K e m p e

### c . 1 3 7 3 - c . 1 4 4 0

*'She could not keep herself from crying and roaring, and this way of crying lasted for many years, in spite of anything anyone could do. The crying was so loud that it astounded people, unless they had heard her before. The more she tried to keep it in, the more she would cry, and the louder.'*

If you visited Lynn in Norfolk in the 1420s, you might have been startled by the sight of a woman weeping and shouting in the street. Her name was Margery Kempe. The lines above are Margery's own description of her weeping, from *The Book of Margery Kempe*. This book was written

The relics that Margery travelled to see were kept in beautiful boxes covered with gold and jewels, called reliquaries. Here Saint Eligius, a famous goldsmith, is making a reliquary.

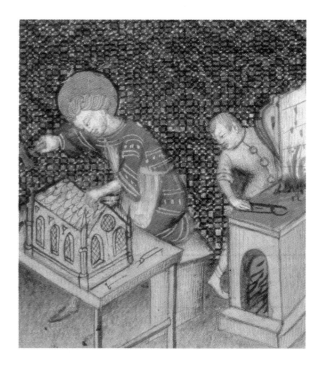

down for her by a priest (like most people of the time, she could not read or write). Although the priest wrote 'She' rather than 'I', most of the words are Margery's own. This book is the first **autobiography** in the English language. It tells the story of a very unusual life.

Margery's weeping was brought on by her strong religious feelings. She only had to see a cross to be reminded of Jesus Christ's suffering and death. Immediately, she would be overcome by 'loud cries and boisterous weepings'. Her neighbours did not know what to make of her. Some said that she was mad, or drunk, or in the power of a devil.

Margery visited Juliana of Norwich to ask for advice. Perhaps they looked like these women, but they would have been separated by a window.

Like Juliana of Norwich, Margery was a mystic. She often felt that she was receiving messages from Christ and the Virgin Mary. But instead of becoming an anchoress, she set off on great journeys which took her all over Europe and to the Middle East.

Margery travelled to **shrines** and holy places. Some shrines held the bodies of saints. Others claimed to have **relics** of Christ, such as drops of his blood or pieces of the cross on which he died. Margery wanted to see as many relics as possible.

Travel was difficult in the Middle Ages and Margery had to put up with many hardships. Sea journeys were dangerous because of the risk of storms and shipwreck. When Margery wanted to go to Spain, she found it hard finding a ship willing to take her. The sailors thought that her weeping would bring bad luck:

*'She prayed that God would keep them from tempests and perils on the sea, so that they might come and go in safety, for she had been told that, if they had a tempest, they would throw her into the sea, for they said it would be her fault.'*

On this map, you can see the great distances that Margery managed to travel on her journeys in search of relics.

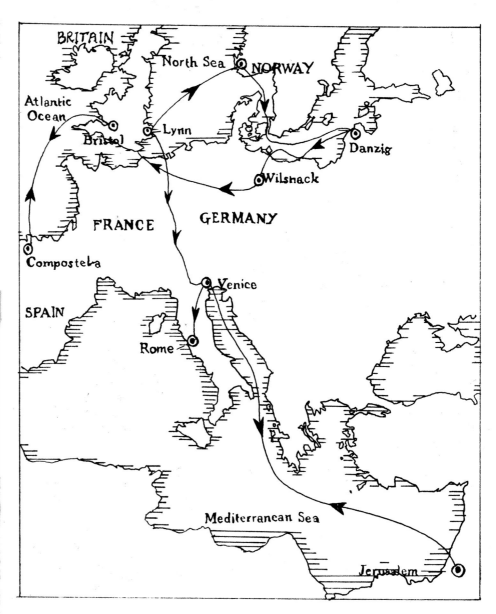

## DATE CHART

**c.1373**
Margery is born in Lynn, later called King's Lynn. She is the daughter of John Burnham, an important citizen and five times mayor of Lynn.

**1393**
Margery marries John Kempe, a local businessman. Over the next twenty years, she gives birth to fourteen children. She also runs a brewery and a mill, though both businesses are unsuccessful.

**1401**
William Sawtry, a priest from Lynn, becomes the first Lollard to be burned at the stake.

**c.1412**
Margery believes that Christ has told her to go to Jerusalem and dress in white. She visits various holy people, including Juliana of Norwich, to ask their advice. She also has to get the permission of her husband and the Bishop of Norwich to leave her family.

**1414**
Margery sets off for Jerusalem. She travels overland to Venice, and then by ship across the Mediterranean.

**1415**
After spending the winter in Rome, Margery returns home.

Land travel was also dangerous, because of the risk of robbery. Whenever possible, people travelled in groups for safety, like Chaucer's pilgrims (see page 28). Margery's problem was finding people who would put up with her crying. Her companions often left her behind.

Although Margery spent so much time on pilgrimages, she did not enjoy travelling abroad. She was terrified of sea voyages and she was not interested in foreign countries. Her book rarely describes any of the places she visited. She went because she wanted to visit the holy shrines, and because she believed that Christ had told her to go. Religion was the only thing she cared about.

Margery's book tells us a lot about the life of women in the Middle Ages. Women who wanted to devote themselves to religion were expected to become nuns or anchoresses, like Juliana of Norwich. Otherwise, women were expected to be housewives and mothers. Margery did not fit

Relics were thought to have the power to cure sick people and people with disabilities. These monks are carrying some relics into a newly built cathedral. You can see two disabled people reaching up towards the relic box.

into either group. She was a mother of fourteen children, yet she dressed in white, a colour worn only by nuns and unmarried women. On her journeys, she met men who said to her:

*'Give up this life that you have chosen. Go home and spin wool, like other women.'*

It was a dangerous time for people who did not fit in. In the early 1400s, English people who disagreed with the Church's teaching, called **Lollards**, were burned at the stake. Margery herself was arrested several times, accused of being a Lollard. She was always found innocent, for she believed everything that the Church taught. It was her strange behaviour that upset people.

This shrine, at Walsingham in Norfolk, was often visited by Margery. It had a famous statue of the Virgin Mary, and what was said to be some milk from Mary's breasts. Rebuilt in the 1930s, the shrine is still visited by pilgrims.

**1417**
**Travels to Santiago de Compostela in Spain to see the tomb of St James. On her return, she goes to see Christ's blood at Hailes Abbey.**

**1417–20**
**Arrested several times as a Lollard. Put on trial at Leicester, York and Beverley, but found innocent.**

**Late 1420s**
**Returns home to nurse her husband, now old and sick. He dies in about 1432.**

**1434**
**Travels to Germany, where she sees Christ's blood in Wilsnack.**

**1432–6**
**Tells her life story to a priest, who writes *The Book of Margery Kempe* for her.**

**c.1440**
**Margery dies, probably in Lynn.**

**1501**
**The printer Wynkyn de Worde publishes some short extracts from Margery's book.**

**1934**
**A complete manuscript of the book is discovered and published for the first time.**

## OTHER MYSTICS

**See page 33**

41

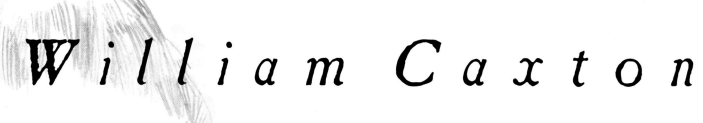

# William Caxton

## c.1421-91

During the Middle Ages, few people in Britain could read and few ever saw a book. In any case, most books were written in Latin, the language of the Church, or French, which was spoken only by rich British people. Books were rare and expensive because they had to be copied by hand. It could take several months to finish a single volume.

By the 1400s, some printers were using wooden blocks to print books. The problem was that every letter of every page had to be carved separately – a very slow process. A great step forward was made in the 1440s by a German **goldsmith** called Johannes Gutenberg. He built a printing press that used separate metal letters. These could be quickly slotted into rows to make up a page. At last it was possible to make hundreds of copies of a book in a short time.

Caxton presents his first book to Margaret, Duchess of Burgundy. The Duchess had encouraged him to write the book, a translation into English of a French story.

The first printed letters were copies of the handwritten letters of the time. Compare these pages, from Caxton's edition of Chaucer's *The Canterbury Tales*, with the handwritten Bible on page 19.

The new invention was brought to Britain by William Caxton. He was a merchant in Bruges, in what is now Belgium. Caxton was also a translator, putting French books into English for wealthy nobles to read. He found that there was a big demand for books in English. To meet this demand, Caxton learned to print.

The arrival of printing changed people's lives in many ways. It became easier for everyone to find out about new ideas and inventions. Printed Bibles helped people to make up their own minds about their religious beliefs, instead of just obeying the Catholic Church. Critics of the Church's teachings could spread their ideas in print. In the 1500s, this led to big areas of northern Europe setting up their own **Protestant** churches.

In the 1550s, one Protestant writer, John Foxe, summed up the changes that printing had brought:

*'Hereby languages are known, knowledge grows ... truth is discovered, falsehood detected. Through printing, the world begins now to have eyes to see and hearts to judge.'*

Printed books even changed the English language. In the Middle Ages, there were big differences between the types of English spoken in different parts of the country. To a northerner, southern English was as hard to understand as French. Caxton helped to change this. Thanks to the new printed books, a standard version of written English was spread – one that could be understood all over the country.

## DATE CHART

**c.1420**
**William Caxton is born in Kent.**

**1446–8**
**Johannes Gutenburg invents a printing press with movable type, and uses it to print a Bible.**

**1471–2**
**Caxton learns how to print in Cologne. He then starts to print books in Bruges.**

**1475**
**Publishes his translation, *The Recuyell of the Historyes of Troye*, the first printed book in English.**

**1476**
**Moves to London and sets up a printing press. Over the next fourteen years, he publishes more than 90 books, including Chaucer's *The Canterbury Tales*.**

**1491**
**Caxton dies.**

## OTHER PRINTERS

**Johannes Gutenberg (c.1390–1468)**
– a German craftsman and printer.
**Laurens Janszoon ('Coster') (1370–1440)**
– a Dutch printer who tried out several new methods.
**Wynkyn de Worde (d. 1534/5)**
– Caxton's assistant who took over the business.

43

# Glossary

**Apprentice** A young beginner, learning a craft. Apprentices had to 'serve' a skilled craftsman for a number of years, in return for their training.

**Archbishop** A leading bishop, who has power over ordinary bishops.

**Autobiography** The life story of someone, written by him or her.

**Becket, St Thomas** Becket (1118–70) was an Archbishop of Canterbury who quarrelled with King Henry II and was murdered by four of Henry's knights.

**Birthright** The right of someone to inherit the throne because of his or her family background.

**Cathedral** A big church which is the head-quarters of a bishop. He has his *cathedra*, or throne, there.

**Catholic Church** The Catholic, or Roman Catholic, Church was the only official church in western Europe throughout the Middle Ages.

**Chancellor** The Chancellor was the most important government minister. He sent out orders and letters from the king.

**Chronicler** A writer of a chronicle, a year-by-year history.

**Expeditions** Organized journeys with a purpose, such as to conquer a land.

**Fortifications** Buildings made for defence, such as city walls and castles.

**Franciscan** A member of an order of friars founded by St Francis of Assisi (1182–1226). Franciscans were supposed to be poor and to live only by begging.

**Friar** A member of a Christian brotherhood set up to spread the Catholic faith. The word 'friar' means brother. Friars were travelling preachers.

**Goldsmith** A worker in gold.

**Heretics** The Church used this word to describe people who held different ideas about religion to the accepted ones.

**Laymen** People who were not priests or monks.

**Lollards** People who rejected the Church's teaching in the 1400s. They said that priests had no special powers, and that many Church activities, including pilgrimages, were worthless.

**Mongols** A warlike people from Mongolia, in Asia. They conquered a huge area of Asia and Eastern Europe in the thirteenth century.

**Monk** A member of a religious brotherhood living in a monastery, also called a priory or an abbey.

**Mystic** A very religious person, to whom people often go for advice.

**Parchment** The skin of a sheep or other animal which was specially prepared for writing on.

**Peasants** Poor people who worked in the countryside, growing food.

**Peasants' Revolt** The rebellion of the peasants, led by Wat Tyler in 1381, against unfair taxes.

**Philosophy** Philosophy means 'wisdom-loving'. Philosophers try to answer the big questions of life, such as the difference between good and evil.

**Pike** A weapon like a spear, with a long metal spike on the end.

**Pilgrims** People who go on religious journeys to holy places.

44

**Priests**  Church officials who look after the day-to-day religious needs of ordinary people.

**Protestant**  The Protestant Churches are those that broke away from the Roman Catholic Church in the 1500s.

**Relics**  Things left behind by saints or other holy people. Relics included saints' bones and items of clothing, and were thought to have special powers.

**Shrines**  A holy place or an object containing something holy, such as the tomb of a saint or a box holding a relic.

**Siege**  An attempt to capture a town or a castle by keeping it surrounded.

**Tower of London**  A fortress on the banks of the River Thames, in London.

**Treasurer**  The minister in charge of the king's money.

**Villeins**  The poorest class of peasants.

**Visions**  Pictures or dreams in the mind.

# *B o o k s   t o   r e a d*

D. Aldred, *Castles and Cathedrals* (Cambridge University Press, 1993)
D. Birkett, *Women and Travel* (Wayland, 1991)
S. and P. Harrison, *Writing and Printing* (BBC Factfinders, 1991)
T. Hosking, *Family Life in Medieval Britain* (Wayland, 1994)
S. Howarth, *Medieval People* (Simon and Schuster, 1991)
N. Hunter, *Medieval Monk* (Wayland, 1987)

J. James, *A Medieval Cathedral* (Simon and Schuster, 1991)
N. Kelly, *The Medieval Realms* (Heinemann Education, 1993)
H. Middleton, *Rulers and Rebels* (Oxford University Press, 1987)
W. Moffat, *A History of Scotland Book Two* (Oxford University Press, 1985)
C. Oaks, *Exploring the Past: Middle Ages* (Hamlyn, 1989)
M. Spankie, *Bruce's Scotland* (Wayland, 1994)

# *P l a c e s   t o   v i s i t*

**Matthew Paris**
St Albans Cathedral, St Albans. Tel: (0727) 860780
The original church attached to the abbey.

**Roger Bacon**
Oxford Tourist Information Centre, Oxford. Tel: (0865) 726871
Oxford still has many buildings and artefacts from the Middle Ages.

**Robert Bruce**
Stirling Castle, Stirling. Tel: (0786) 450000
Robert Bruce won his greatest victory outside this castle.

**John Wycliffe**
Balliol College, Oxford. Tel: (0865) 277777
The college where Wycliffe was a teacher.

**Wat Tyler**
Blackheath, London. Tel: Greenwich Tourist Information Centre (081) 858 6376

**Henry Yeveley and Geoffrey Chaucer**
Canterbury Cathedral, Canterbury. Tel: (0227) 762862

**Juliana of Norwich**
The Julian Centre, Norwich. Tel: (0603) 767380
You can see a modern reconstruction of Juliana's anchorhold at St Julian's Church.

**Owain Glyndwr**
Harlech Castle, Harlech. Tel: (0766) 780552
Harlech Castle was captured by Glyndwr, who held it from 1404-8.

**Margery Kempe**
St Margaret's Church, King's Lynn. Tel: (0553) 772858
The church where Kempe prayed and worshipped.

**William Caxton**
Science Museum, London. Tel: (071) 938 8000
Gallery of paper and printing.

# I n d e x